Math on the Job

Math at the Vet

Tracey Steffora

Heinemann
LIBRARY

Chicago, Illinois

Edited by Dan Nunn and Abby Colich
Designed by Victoria Allen
Picture research by Tracy Cummins
Production control by Vicki Fitzgerald

Printed and bound in China by Leo Paper Group

15 14 13 12
10 9 8 7 6 5 4 3 2 1

Library of Congress Cataloging-in-Publication Data
Steffora, Tracey.
  Math at the vet / Tracey Steffora.—1st ed.
    p. cm.—(Math on the job)
  Includes bibliographical references and index.
  ISBN 978-1-4329-7155-7 (hb)—ISBN 978-1-4329-7162-5
(pb) 1. Veterinarians—Juvenile literature. 2. Mathematics—
Juvenile literature. I. Title.

SF756.S74 2013
636.089—dc23   2012013380

Acknowledgments
The author and publishers are grateful to the following for
permission to reproduce copyright material: Corbis: pp. 7
(© Ocean), 11 (© Corbis); Getty Images: pp. 5 (John Wood
Photography), 12 (MICHAEL URBAN/AFP), 15 (Vstock LLC),
18 (John Wood Photography), 19 (Thinkstock), 20 (LWA);
iStockphoto: pp. 4 (© kali9), 14 (© Alina Solovyova-Vincent),
16 (© Miodrag Gajic), 22b (© Alina Solovyova-Vincent);
Shutterstock: pp. 6 (Eric Isselée), 8 (Vladislav Pavlovich),
10 (Mark William Penny), 13 (Pixel Memoirs), 17 (Utekhina
Anna), 22a (erashov); Superstock: pp. 9 (© Minden Pictures),
21 (© Kablonk).

Front cover photograph a veterinarian examining a bulldog
puppy reproduced with permission from Getty Images
(Photographer's Choice).

Back cover photograph of a veterinarian with ferret
reproduced with permission from Shutterstock (Vladislav
Pavlovich).

Every effort has been made to contact copyright holders
of any material reproduced in this book. Any omissions will
be rectified in subsequent printings if notice is given to the
publisher.

Contents

Math at the Vet

A vet is a doctor for animals.

A vet uses math every day.

Size

Animals are different sizes.

This animal is big.

This animal is small.

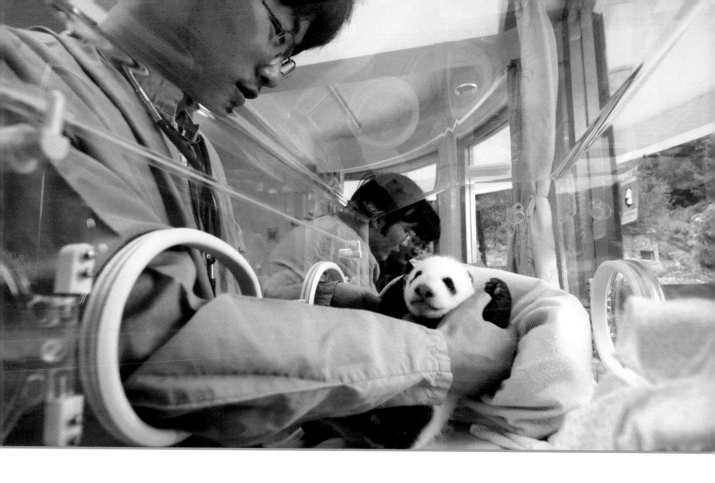

Is this animal big or small?

(answer on page 22)

Measuring

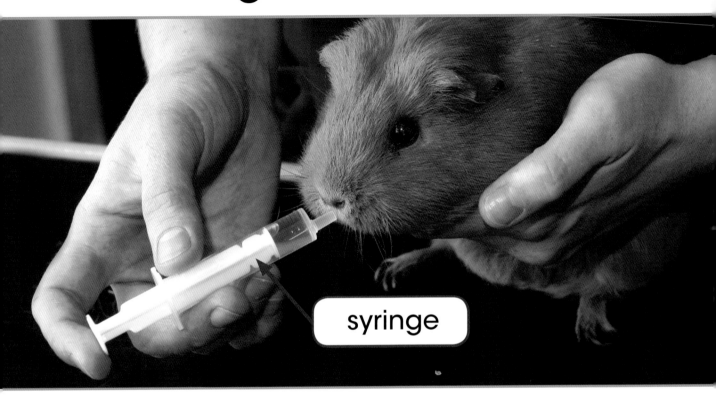

syringe

The vet measures how much.

scale

The vet measures how heavy.

The vet measures how long.

Which is taller? The cat or the dog?

(answer on page 22)

Counting

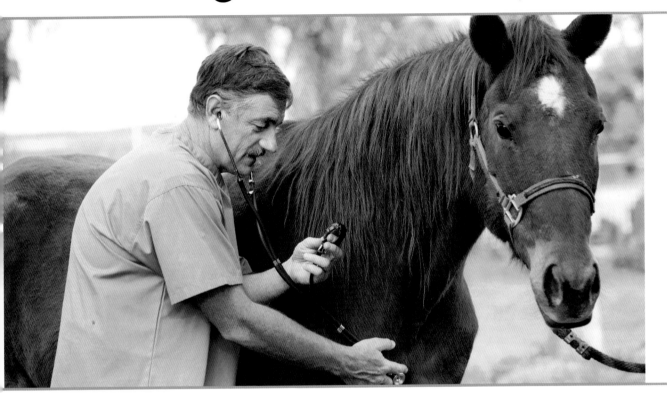

The vet counts heartbeats.

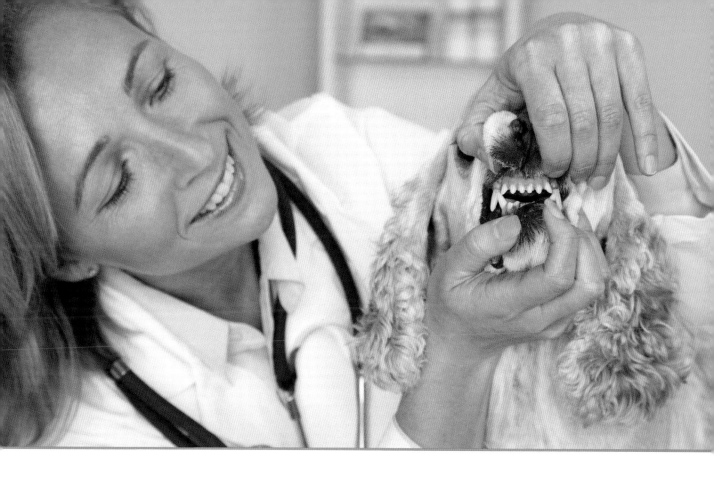

The vet counts teeth.

The vet counts puppies.

How many kittens are there?

(answer on page 22)

17

Time

The vet sees many animals.

The vet sees one animal at a time.

clock

A clock shows what time it is.

Schedule

Time	Name	Animal
8:00 a.m.	Rover	dog
8:30 a.m.	Fluffy	cat
9:00 a.m.	Patches	rabbit
9:30 a.m.	Bob	cat

What time will the vet see Fluffy?

(answer on page 22)

Answers

page 9: The animal is small.

page 13: The dog is taller.

page 17: There are five kittens.

page 21: The vet will see Fluffy at 8:30 a.m. (a.m. means in the morning).

Picture Glossary

clock object used for measuring and telling time

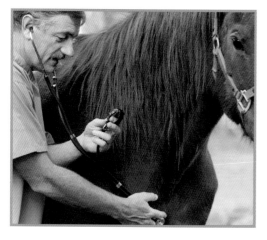

heartbeat sounds that happens when the heart pumps blood

Index

Notes for parents and teachers

Math is a way that we make sense of the world around us. For the young child, this includes recognizing similarities and differences, classifying objects, recognizing shapes and patterns, developing number sense, and using simple measurement skills.

Before reading

Connect with what children know.

Discuss what a veterinarian does and allow children to share any experience they have had caring for animals or taking animals to the vet's office.

After reading

Build upon children's curiosity and desire to explore.

Identify some of the different tools that a vet uses, such as a scale, stethoscope, thermometer, and ruler. Discuss what these tools measure, and have children look through other books about vets to identify pictures of these tools being used.

Have children name animals they are familiar with. Ask questions that encourage comparison such as: "Which is taller, a cow or a chicken?" and "Do you think a cat or a horse has a longer tail?"